Having Fun with
PAPER

Sarah Medina

WAYLAND

First published in 2007 by Wayland

Copyright © Wayland 2007

Wayland
338 Euston Road
London NW1 3BH

Wayland
Hachette Children's Books
Level 17/207 Kent Street
Sydney, NSW 2000

Medina, Sarah
  Having fun with paper. – (Let's do art)
  1. Paper work – Juvenile literature
  I. Title
  745.5'4

WILTSHIRE	
C745.54	PETERS
04-Feb-2009	

Written by Sarah Medina
Produced by Calcium
Design and model making by Emma DeBanks
Photography by Tudor Photography
Consultancy and concepts by Lisa Regan

ISBN 978-0-7502-4893-8

Printed in China

Wayland is a division of Hachette Children's Books.

Contents

Paper Fun!

Paper can be used in lots of ways! You can cut it, fold it, scrunch it, weave it, paint it and glue it to make all sorts of projects. You will need several different types of paper to make the projects in this book.

- Cardboard
- Cardboard rolls
- Cereal box
- Coloured card
- Coloured paper
- Magazines
- Metallic paper
- Paper plates

- Tissue paper
- White paper
- White stickers
- Lots of different scraps of paper and cardboard

Note for adults
Children may need adult assistance with some of the project steps. Turn to page 23 for Further Ideas and for a recipe for *papier mâché* paste.

Read the 'You will need' boxes carefully for a full list of what you need to make each project.

Before you start, ask an adult to:

• find a surface where you can make the projects.

• find an apron to cover your clothes, or some old clothes that can get messy.

• do things, such as cutting with scissors, that are a little tricky to do on your own.

Picture of Me!

You can use paper to make a picture of yourself!

You will need
- Paper and card in different colours
- Tissue paper or metallic paper
- Pencil
- Scissors
- PVA glue

1 Look in a mirror and see what shape your face, eyes, nose and mouth are. Draw your face shape on card, and cut it out.

2 Cut strips of tissue paper or metallic paper for hair and glue them around the face.

3 Draw eyes on card, cut them out and glue them onto the face.

5 Draw a mouth on card, cut it out and glue it onto the face.

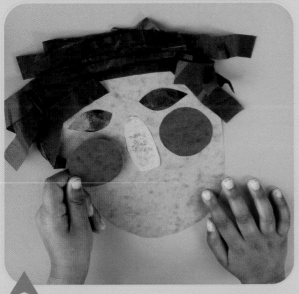

4 Draw a nose and cheeks on card, cut them out and glue them onto the face.

 Ask an adult to help you when cutting card!

Concertina Bracelet

Wear this pretty bracelet
to a party!

You will need
- 2 narrow strips of card in different colours, 60cm long
- PVA glue

2 Glue one end of each strip together, as shown in the photo.

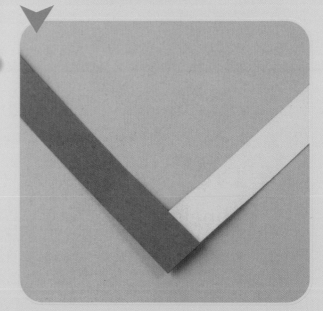

1 Take two strips of brightly coloured card.

3 Carefully fold the first strip across the other strip, and press down firmly.

4 Now fold the second strip across the first strip, and keep folding until the strips are folded right to the end.

5 Glue the two ends of the folded strips together, and put your bracelet on.

Flower Shapes

Make beautiful wrapping paper using cut-out flower shapes. You could use it to cover a notebook.

You will need
- I circle of white paper
- I sheet of dark paper
- Sponge
- Poster paints
- Scissors

1 Fold a paper circle in half, then in half again and then again.

2 Draw shapes on the edges of the paper wedge and cut them out.

3 Open up your flower shape and place it on dark paper.

4 Put paint on the sponge and dab it gently over the flower.

 Ask an adult to help you when cutting paper!

5 Lift up the flower shape, move it across the paper and dab paint on it again. Repeat as many times as you like to make a pretty pattern!

Colourful Mat

Brighten up your bedside table with this colourful mat.

You will need
- 1 sheet of coloured paper
- Strips of paper in bright colours
- Pencil
- Scissors
- Sticky tape

1 Draw and cut out a square from the sheet of paper.

2 Draw straight lines across the paper and make slits by cutting along the lines. Do not cut right to the edge of the paper.

3 Starting at the top, weave a coloured strip of paper in and out of the slits.

5 Turn your mat over and tape down the edges.

4 Keep weaving the coloured strips of paper in and out of the slits until you reach the bottom.

 Ask an adult to help you when cutting paper!

Notice Board

Make a notice board to help you remember what you need to do!

You will need
- 1 whiteboard
- 1 whiteboard marker pen
- 1 sheet of white circle-shape stickers
- Felt-tip pens

1 Draw and colour faces onto some of the circle-shaped stickers.

2 Draw and colour other patterns onto the rest of the stickers.

14

3 Peel off a sticker and stick it onto one edge of the whiteboard.

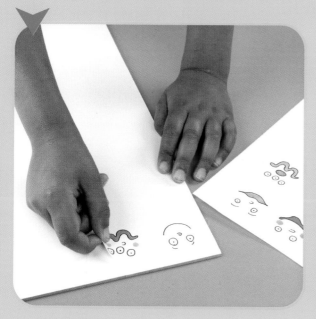

4 Stick the rest of the stickers around the edges of the whiteboard until you have gone all the way round.

5 Using the whiteboard marker pen, draw a picture or make a note on your notice board.

Flower Garland

This pretty flower garland will brighten up any room!

1 Thread beads onto each end of the pipe cleaners, and fold the ends over to hold the beads in place.

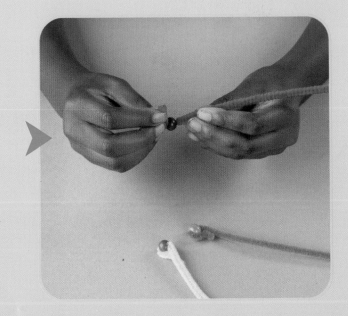

2 Bend each pipe cleaner in half.

3 Cut strips of tissue paper to make flowers.

5 Tape the finished flowers onto a piece of string, and hang your flower garland up!

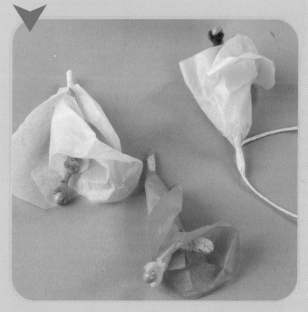

4 Roll the strips of tissue paper around the pipe cleaners and beads, and secure them with tape.

 Ask an adult to help you when cutting tissue paper!

17

Day and Night Clock

Practise telling the time with this clock of two halves!

You will need

- 1 empty cereal box
- 2 paper plates
- 2 paper fasteners
- Cardboard
- Felt-tip pen
- Paintbrush
- Pencil
- Poster paints
- PVA glue
- Scissors

1 Paint one half of a cereal box yellow and the other side black.

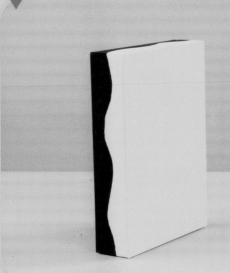

 Ask an adult to help you when cutting and using paper fasteners!

2 Draw a clock face onto each plate. Glue one clock onto each side of the box.

3 Draw two long hands and two short hands onto the cardboard, and cut them out.

4 Fasten the hands onto the middle of each clock.

5 Paint a sun and flowers onto the daytime clock, and a moon and stars onto the night-time clock.

Scary Monster

Get together with a friend and make the scariest monster you can think of!

You will need
- 1 round balloon
- 1 coloured pom-pom
- 3 ping-pong balls
- Strips of paper from magazines
- 2 cardboard rolls
- 1 sheet of card
- *Papier mâché* paste (see page 23)
- Felt-tip pen
- Paintbrush
- Pencil
- Poster paints
- PVA glue
- Scissors

1 Blow up a balloon and tie a knot in the end. Tear strips of paper from magazines and, using *papier mâché* paste, glue paper strips all over the balloon. Leave to dry. Repeat twice.

2 Draw a wavy mouth shape onto card, cut it out and glue it onto the monster's face.

3 Glue a pom-pom onto the monster's face to make a nose.

4 Paint the cardboard rolls to make the monster's legs, and leave to dry.

5 Cut slits around both ends of the cardboard rolls, and open them up.

 Do not blow balloons up too much. They might burst!

21

6 Glue the monster's legs onto the body.

7 Using a felt-tip pen, draw little circles in the middle of the ping-pong balls, and glue them onto the monster's head, for eyes.

Further Ideas

Once a child has finished the projects in *Having Fun with Paper*, they can add some other exciting finishing touches to them. Here are some suggestions for each project:

Picture of Me!
Make a hat to add to the portrait! Cut out a hat from card, and decorate it with brightly coloured paints and sequins.

Concertina Bracelet
Make more bracelets in different colours and give them out as friendship tokens. Add stick-on gems to the bracelets to make them precious!

Flower Shapes
Add some glue to the paper and sprinkle glitter over it to make it sparkle.

Colourful Mat
Make a mat for each member of the family in their favourite colours, and use them at the meal table. If you have access to a laminating machine, you can make them waterproof.

Notice Board
Use letter stickers to add the words DON'T FORGET along the top or bottom of the board.

Flower Garland
Use green paper to make leaf shapes to add to the flower garland.

Day and Night Clock
Decorate the clocks and the box with shiny shapes cut from metallic paper and with colourful sequins.

Scary Monster
Give the monster some hair. Cut out and paint strips of paper in bright colours, then glue them to the monster's head.

How to make *papier mâché* paste
Stir equal amounts of PVA glue and water in an old container with a lid. The paste will last for several days if you keep the lid on.

Further Information

With access to the Internet, you can check out several helpful websites for further arts and crafts ideas for young children.

www.bbc.co.uk/cbeebies/artbox/artisttips/
www.bbc.co.uk/cbeebies/artbox/doodledo/makes/
www.kidsart.com/q82700.html
www.avalon-arts.com/studio/paper.html
www.enchantedlearning.com/crafts/papercrafts/
www.makingfriends.com/precrafts.htm

Glossary

garland a long string of flowers or leaves used for decoration

metallic shiny and sparkly, like silver or gold

papier mâché a paste of glue and shredded paper which sets hard when dry

tissue paper thin, almost see-through craft paper

weave thread strips of paper, fabric or other materials in lines going in opposite directions, to make a solid piece of work

Index